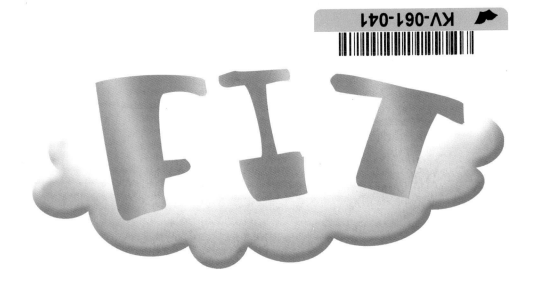

Author: Lisa Regan
Consultant: Dr. Kristina Routh

www.mileskelly.net

First published in 2005 by Miles Kelly Publishing Ltd
Bardfield Centre Great Bardfield Essex CM7 4SL

2 4 6 8 10 9 7 5 3 1

British Library Cataloguing-in-Publication Data
A catalogue record for this book is available from the
British Library

ISBN 1-84236-555-X

Printed in Thailand

Publishing Director: Anne Marshall
Editor: Teresa Putnam
Designer: Louisa Leitao
Picture Research: Laura Faulder, Liberty Newton
Production Manager: Estela Boulton
Colour Separation: Miles Kelly Publishing

www.mileskelly.net
info@mileskelly.net

Contents

Introduction

Fit is jam-packed with handy hints, tips and information!

Info, Info, Info!

Learn how certain foods are good for you, and why some should be avoided. Find exercises or sports that take your fancy, and keep you bursting with energy! Discover how healthy-living can improve your overall appearance and self-confidence. Then it's onto the more serious stuff! Find out about career choices, part-time work, staying safe, hormones, body changes and relationships.

Saint or Sinner?

Follow the devil and angel for vital 'dos' and 'don'ts' and a summary of important information that has been taken from each section of the book. Use these tips to see if you're a saint or a sinner!

A Girl's Best Friend!

Not only that, but there's also a fun diary for your use! You can jot down anything from events or schoolwork to secrets or your thoughts and feelings each day.
Or, if the information in this book leaves you in a pro-active mood, full of get-up-and-go, then you can use the diary to record your daily food and exercise routines:
✫ Apple column – record how much fruit and veg you eat each day.
✫ Trainer column – write down how many minutes of exercise you do.
✫ Glass column – jot down how many glasses of water you drink.

Help's at Hand!

If you find you're left wanting more information, more advice and more discussion on a topic, check out the 'Ask For Help' features found on some pages. These offer advice about who to turn to for more info.

The Fun Stuff!

But fear not! It's not all learning, learning, learning. Fit is fun and interactive with entertaining quizzes and flowcharts that you can enjoy doing by yourself or with friends.

Get Going, Girl!

So what's stopping you, girl? Get reading, get going, get FIT!

Healthy Eating

Shopping List
6 Apples
2 Bananas
3 Oranges
Pasta

A Fruitful Life

Do you know how much fruit and veg you eat in a day? Do you know how much you should eat?

The answer to the second question is simple: follow the 'five-a-day' plan, which means you eat five portions of fruit and veg every day. There's more of that below. According to recent surveys, children of school-age eat less than half the amount they should.

Why Bother?

Fruit and veg are vital for your body and brain. They help you fight off illnesses. They're low in fat, so you can fill up on fruit and veg, rather than eating fatty or sugary foods. If you eat your five-a-day, you should start to feel great. Otherwise your skin, hair, nails and teeth will look bad and you'll have less energy and smelly breath!

Five-A-Day

The good news is that fruit juice and salads count towards your five-a-day too! See page 16 for information on what a portion is. Be sure to vary your diet regularly because if your diet isn't varied enough, you still won't get the goodness you need, regardless of how much healthy food you're eating.

The Rules

Follow these rules, to help you eat the right stuff without even thinking about it.

1 It's all about balance. No foods are completely good or completely bad. You can still eat burgers, crisps or cakes as a treat every now and then.

2 The more calories you put in your body, the more energy you need to burn off. Check out pages 28–29 for everyday exercises to use up calories and tone your muscles.

3 Less is more. You don't have to eat 'til you're stuffed! If you're full after two slices of pizza, don't eat a third.

Eat your favourite foods... just don't pig out!

All About Balance

Sorry, nothing to do with piles of profiteroles, but everything to do with having a balanced diet.

Check out this picture. Do some of the foods look more appetising than others? Hopefully, you're drawn to the healthy foods, such as fruit and veg. You're supposed to eat more of these foods every day. Sugars and fats are treats. That means once a day and not your main source of food!

Fill-You-Up Foods
Fibre foods, such as potatoes, rice, cereals (wheat, oats), and products containing them, such as bread or pasta, should be your staple food throughout the day.

Dairy
Dairy products are a great source of protein as they also provide calcium and some vitamins.

Protein
Proteins can come from meat, fish, milk or eggs. Seeds and pulses, such as lentils or beans, are vital substitutes for vegetarians.

Sugar and Fats
Too much sugar and fat is bad for your teeth, your heart, your weight and your energy levels.

Fruit and Veg
You should already know how important fruit and veg is to help maintain a healthy diet.

In Moderation

Eating healthily doesn't mean that you have to chop out all your fave foods. If you love a plate of burger and chips, or crave chocolate, then you can still eat them. The key thing is to balance these foods with healthier ones. When you eat 'junk food' be sure to eat something nutritious and healthy earlier or later that day.

Don't Diet

If you're eating the right balance you shouldn't need to eat lots of 'diet' products. Check food labels carefully; for example low-fat yoghurts may have more sugar than the full fat versions!

> **Do...** eat lots of foods containing fibre – it's good for your digestion.

> **Don't...** binge on one meal. Eat little and often to keep your blood sugar levels healthy.

How Much of Each?

If you don't eat enough, your body switches to 'starvation mode' and tries to use as little fuel as it can to maintain your energy stores. That's why it's best to eat regular, healthy meals. Your daily target should be to eat five servings of the fill-you-up (fibre) foods, five of fruit and veg, two to three of protein, and one from the sugars and fats.

Get the Balance Right

Scientists developed the food groups to help you eat the right amounts of each food type. Even though lots of fats or sugars are bad for you, having a small amount of each in your diet helps your body to function properly. Remember that these food groups are cunningly hidden in lots of the foods you eat. Many foods are cooked in fat, or have some fat added to make them seem tastier. Sugar occurs naturally in many foods, including milk and fruit, and is often added to pre-prepared food. If you're keen to know exactly what goes into your meals, you can try cooking them from scratch yourself. Get someone to help you, and make it fun!

Top To Toe

Your body is an amazing piece of machinery, made up of hundreds of working parts.

To keep yourself operating to your full potential, you need to take care of every bit of your bod.

Working Girl

Check out this picture. The labels point to just some of the parts of your body, in particular the main internal organs. The list on page 13 briefly explains what you need to include in your diet to ensure that each of these parts is kept in good working condition. It can't be said enough – a balanced and nutritious diet is essential to maintain a healthy body. Add to that plenty of fresh air and exercise (see pages 22–25 for some ideas of what activities to do) and get plenty of beauty sleep (see page 41) and you'll probably be fit for anything!

ASK FOR...

HELP!

Family History

Find out about your family's medical history. Some illnesses can be hereditary (passed down from relatives) and in some cases, a slight change in diet can help prevent such diseases or problems in later life.

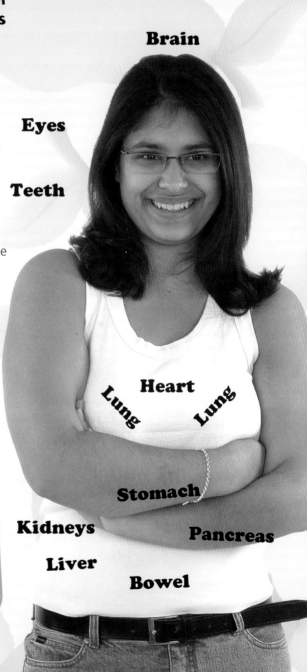

Brain

Eyes

Teeth

Heart

Lung

Lung

Stomach

Kidneys

Pancreas

Liver

Bowel

Bones	Adults have 206 bones in their body. You need a good daily supply of calcium (from dairy foods, such as milk and butter). This helps to keep all of them strong and healthy.
Bowel	Your digestive system helps to extract goodness from food and expels the waste products. You should eat fibre (such as wholemeal bread and pasta), beans and eggs to keep in tiptop condition.
Brain	Make sure you eat enough fat, especially from oily fish, such as salmon, pilchards and mackerel (but only up to two portions a week). Oily fish can help to increase your IQ and concentration.
Eyes	It's not a myth – carrots really do help to improve your eyesight, including your night vision! That's because they contain vitamin A, which helps to form the light-sensitive parts of your eyes.
Heart	Your heart can be affected by the cholesterol in your blood. To maintain a healthy cholesterol level, cut out saturated fats (found in junk food and animal fats, such as fatty products, for example cream).
Kidneys	Your kidneys control the water and mineral levels in your blood. You may need to alter your diet if you have kidney problems, such as those caused by having diabetes.
Liver	Your liver helps with digesting food and keeping your blood healthy. A high-fibre, low-salt eating pattern keeps your liver functioning at its best. Alcohol is particularly bad for your liver.
Lungs	Your lungs are the main part of your respiratory (breathing) system, and are badly affected by smoking cigarettes. You can help them stay healthier by eating nuts, margarine and wholegrain cereals.
Pancreas	Your pancreas makes insulin to control your blood sugar levels. If these levels fall quickly, you'll feel low in energy and even your spirits can drop. Keep your blood sugars level by eating little and often.
Skin	A good supply of vitamins A, B3 (niacin) and C all help to keep your skin healthy. These are found in liver, oily fish, citrus and other orange or yellow fruits and veg, strawberries and potatoes.
Stomach	Your stomach works best if it's fed little and often, so it always has some food in it. Eating a healthy snack between mealtimes can help prevent the production of too much acid in the stomach.
Teeth	Too much sugar and starch can lead to tooth decay. Your teeth are at their most vulnerable in your youth. After the age of about 25 your tooth enamel is harder and more resistant.

Water, Water

Nearly three-quarters of the body is made up of water. So, it's surprising we don't trickle away into the mattress overnight!

Seriously, though, if our water levels drop we start to feel bad. Think of an unwatered plant, withered and drooping on the window sill. That's how you'll feel if you don't have enough fluid inside.

How Much?

You should try to drink eight medium glasses of water each day – more if the weather's hot or if you're exercising. You can drink tap water with ice and lemon in it, or bottled water (fizzy or still are fine). If you're not keen on plain water, try weak diluted squash or some fresh fruit juice with it. Beware coffee and cola, as their high caffeine levels just make you wee more, so you're losing the fluid you've taken in.

Alternative Medicine

Headaches, nausea and dizziness are sometimes your body's way of telling you that you're becoming dehydrated (lacking in water). Instead of taking a tablet, first drink two glasses of water and see if your symptoms ease. Another clue of mild dehydration is if your wee is a very dark yellow colour.

But Why?

Water has some major functions in your body, including controlling your body temperature and moving nutrients, oxygen and waste products through your system. Water's also great for making your skin glow, your eyes gleam and stopping you from gaining excess weight.

Juicy Booster!

A glass of warm water with lemon squeezed into it is a great way to kick start your system in the morning!

What's Organic?

There's a lot of talk about 'eating organic', but what *is* organic food?

Organic refers to the way food is grown, bred or processed. No chemicals, such as fertilizers and pesticides, are used on organic crops. Instead, organic farming is an ecological system that relies on rich, healthy soil to produce plants strong enough to resist pests and diseases.

GM Foods

GM stands for 'genetically-modified' and involves scientific manipulation of crops to change their characteristics. Previously, crops were cross-bred to improve their taste, size, appearance and strength. GM crops have been scientifically 'fast-tracked' to make the same adjustments. Organic farming doesn't allow this kind of modification.

What's Best?

There is much debate about this subject. There isn't conclusive evidence that organic crops are healthier to eat, although supporters say that the food tastes better. They say that with non-organic foods, appearance is more important than taste. For example, supermarkets buy tomatoes that are all the same size and shape, even if they don't taste as good. There is also the fear that chemicals used in farming can't be removed before the food is eaten, and these chemicals may be harmful to humans and the environment over a long period of time. Many people are opposed to genetically-modified foods because they believe in maintaining a natural state of crop-growing, which promotes a balance in the environment.

Genetically Modified

Organic

Feeling Fruity

As you've read already, fruit and veg are a vital part of your diet.

Not to mention they're easy to pack in your lunchbox, and great dipped in salsa or hummus. For a yummy and healthy dessert, chop up three or four kinds of fruit to make a colourful fruit salad. Tick off each of the fruits and vegetables in the box on this page as you eat them, and try to vary which ones you have each day. For each item on the list it tells you what counts as one portion towards your five-a-day target.

Item	How Many?
☐ Apple	One medium
☐ Banana	One medium
☐ Broccoli	Two large pieces
☐ Brussels sprouts	Four
☐ Cabbage	Half cup
☐ Carrot	One medium
☐ Cauliflower	Half cup
☐ Celery	Two medium stalks
☐ Cherries	Ten
☐ Cucumber	Half cup sliced
☐ Grapefruit	Half medium
☐ Grapes	About 18
☐ Green peas	Half cup
☐ Juice	One small glass*
☐ Lettuce	Half cup
☐ Nectarine	One medium
☐ Orange	One medium
☐ Peach	One medium
☐ Pear	One medium
☐ Pepper	Half cup chopped
☐ Pineapple	Half cup chopped
☐ Plum	One medium
☐ Raisins	Quarter cup
☐ Radishes	About five
☐ Raspberries	13 medium
☐ Strawberries	About seven medium
☐ Sweetcorn	Half cup
☐ Tomato	Half cup, cubed

* Only one portion a day counts

Smoothie Fun!

If you have a food processor or blender ask a grown-up to check that it's clean and safe to use. Then throw in your fave fruits and concoct your own smoothies – add yoghurt, milk or fruit juice for extra calcium and vitamins.

Help's At Hand

An alarming number of people worry about their weight, or how 'fat' they think they might be.

Sadly, many people think they need to lose weight to be happy, attractive to others, or successful. Being overweight can cause health problems. If you're concerned about your weight, you can see a school nurse or doctor for advice on increasing the amount of exercise you do or for ways to adapt your diet to eat healthily and responsibly.

Eating Disorders

Many people suffer from illnesses that affect their eating habits. Anorexia nervosa is a condition where the person tries to starve themselves. Some try to control their weight by vomiting, over-exercising or taking laxatives (bulimia nervosa). Others constantly eat too much and feel guilty about it (binge-eating disorder).

What You Can Do

If you suspect that a friend suffers from an eating disorder, talk to them about it, or seek advice from someone else. If you talk directly to your friend first, don't insist that they have a problem. Say you're worried about their eating habits, and are scared it could lead to a problem. Then listen to what they have to say. Talking to you about it might help them face their problem.

Get More Help

If your friend asks you to, go with them to see a grown-up, such as a teacher, parent or doctor, to talk about things further. If your friend asks you to keep it a secret, gently explain to them that some things need to be talked about and that as their true friend you can't keep your worries inside. It's for their own good, and for your good too, as you could make yourself ill by carrying a burden like this.

Healthy Eating – Saint or Sinner?

Don't...

✿ have too much sugar and fat in your diet – limit these to treats or to sweeten other healthier food or drink
✿ skip meals or snack on junk food
✿ 'crash' diet, or eat irresponsibly, so that your food intake is imbalanced

Do...

✿ eat at least five portions of fruit and veg every day
✿ eat a balanced diet, with fibre, proteins, calcium and some sugars
✿ drink plenty of water every day to keep your body functioning properly

Are You Food Savvy?

See how much you know about healthy eating!

1 Which has more vitamin C?
a. Portion of strawberries
b. Whole orange

2 Which party snack is the healthiest option?
a. Crisps
b. Raw mixed nuts
c. Cocktail sausages
d. Blue cheese and tomato vol-au-vents

3 Which of these is the least healthiest option for a snack between meals?
a. Glass of milk, celery and salsa dip
b. Fruit juice and peanut butter sarnie
c. Drinking yoghurt and cheese toastie
d. Water, rice cakes and hummus dip

4 Which two of these calcium foods are also fattening?
a. Butter
b. Cheese
c. Spinach
d. Dried apricots

5 Ideally, how many times should you eat throughout the day?
a. Three times: brekkie, lunch, dinner
b. Have a snack or meal every three to four hours
c. Whenever you're hungry
d. Lots in the morning, less in the afternoon, nothing after 6.00 p.m.

6 Which fruit has the most sugar?
a. Plums
b. Apples
c. Bananas

7 Which foods are particularly good for your teeth?
a. Nuts
b. Milk
c. Cheese
d. Apples

8 You're feeling rather icky and can't face food. What's your best bet?
a. Ginger biscuits
b. Chocolate
c. Milkshake

ANSWERS: 1 a; **2** b; **3** c is a bit of a protein overload, so have water or juice instead and add tomato to your toastie; **4** a and b; **5** b is right for a growing person, because your stomach can't hold enough to provide nutrients, energy and brain-food if you only eat three times a day. **6** c; **7** all except d; **8** a – ginger can stop queasiness.

Diet Diary

Use this table to keep a note of what you eat in a week. You might be surprised!

Photocopy it if you want to keep a more continuous record of your eating habits.

Don't fool yourself – write down every single thing you eat. Can you honestly say you eat five portions of fruit and veg each day? Underline all the food that is high in fat or energy (see page 10 for these foods) to see if you are eating too many.

	Breakfast	Lunch	Dinner	Snacks	Drinks
Monday					
Tuesday					
Wednesday					
Thursday					
Friday					
Saturday					
Sunday					

keeping
Fit

Timetable

Thursday	Friday	Saturday	Sunday
Horse Riding 4pm		Ballet 11am	
	Swimming 5.30pm		Bike ride with Hannah 2pm

Fitness... The Facts

Hey you! Did you say getting fit is boring? I don't think so... only real dummies think that.

Keeping fit is essential if you want to have strong bones, toned muscles and a healthy heart, and there are lots of ways to do it if you're not a gym-babe.

> **Do...**
> small things each day to keep fit, such as taking stairs instead of lifts.

Miss Universe

You won't become Miss Universe by cycling once a week! It's a fact that females are born with less muscle than men, and have less testosterone (the hormone related to muscle growth). Exercise can tone your muscles to make them more shapely.

> **Don't...**
> push yourself too much. Over-stretching can cause injury.

No Pain, No Gain

Pain is not a good thing when you're exercising, as it's the sign of an injury. The kind of pain you might get from exercise is simply tiredness, or maybe a few stiff muscles the next day if you're new to it. This shows that you're working hard enough to see a slight improvement in your strength, shape and health.

Back to Basics

Here are the basic health reasons for doing regular exercise.

1 Regular exercise promotes cardiovascular (heart) fitness and increases your overall health.

2 Exercise prevents you becoming overweight, which can have all sorts of health implications.

3 The impact helps to keep your bones strong. For example, jogging is better for your bones than walking.

4 The more you use your muscles, the bigger they get – and bigger muscles use more calories even when resting.

Decision Time

So, you want to get fitter, but you don't want to spend hours on a running machine... zzzzzzzz!

Don't stress, there are lots of other options that are much more fun.

Martial Arts

Karate, judo or tae kwan do are just some of the martial arts on offer. If you fancy trying something a little different, it's worth finding out what martial arts classes are held locally. High-energy martial arts help build speed, strength and stamina. Classes of any kind are a good way to make new friends, too. However, you may only find the time to go to one class a week so try other activities alongside your martial arts.

Team Sports

You probably either love 'em or hate 'em. If you do love team sports, such as netball, hockey, football or volleyball, then join a local team. You'll get the benefits of structured training sessions, at least one game a week, plus a group of friends outside school. Not bad for an hour or so running around like a crazy woman!

Fit For Free

Not all exercise has to cost money! If you want to do some fitness, but don't have the pennies for surfing or skiing, try these!

1 Wherever possible, take the stairs instead of a lift or escalator.

2 If it's a safe route and you're allowed, walk to school. Recruit a friend to join you and you can have a good gossip along the way!

3 If you have a dog, walk it! If not, join a friend in walking theirs. Trips down the park with siblings can be great fun and good exercise.

Cycling

If you haven't got a bike, borrow one! Then talk a friend into joining you. Cycling is eco-friendly, great exercise and cheaper than the bus. You can burn at least 300 calories cycling for an hour at a steady rate, plus your heart and lungs will be healthier and your legs will look firmer. Sounds fab!

Use your head... wear a helmet!

Horse Riding

Horse riding will exercise muscles you didn't even know existed! The posture needed for horse riding will firm your bum and thighs, and strengthen your back and hips. Make sure that you go to a reputable riding school, which will help you to learn to ride safely.

Skateboarding

Skateboarding is a great way to get fresh air and new friends. As long as you wear protective gear, and avoid injuries, such as sprains, skateboarding is great for raising your heart rate, strengthening your knee and ankle joints, and giving your leg muscles a good workout.

Rollerblading

Grab some protective pads, a helmet and a friend, find a park and away you go! Rollerblading raises your heart rate, and is low-impact if you're worried about previous injuries. Remember to stay safe – don't skate alone at night, or in isolated spots, and make sure an adult knows your whereabouts.

Gymnastics

Gymnasts are slim, supple and strong, with great balance, posture and coordination skills. Gymnastics has also been proven to improve bone density more than any other sport. Not bad for a few cartwheels and some handsprings! Plus, as you get better at it, a backflip is a fab party trick!

Get Out And About

Check out these if none of the previous sports grabbed you.

They'll give you an excuse to get some fresh air! So grab some mates and get going…

Swimming

Swimming is a great way to free your mind of stress and worries and lift your spirits, while giving your muscles a good workout. The buoyancy you get from the water eases the strain on your joints, making it great for people who are unfit when they start out. If you want to burn calories you'll have to swim quite a lot at a steady speed, but always start and finish with a few slow lengths. Get a friend to tag along and you can even chat between lengths!

Surfing

Woah, dude! Surfing really is an all-round fab activity. It's great for your image, tan, health and fitness. Paddling out on your board into the water strengthens your upper body, and riding the waves back in tones your lower body. Try balancing on your board to start; you'll notice your muscles the next day! To top it all, the balance and concentration needed are great skills to master.

Skiing

Skiing and snowboarding build the strength in your legs and back, and get your heart pumping. However, make sure you're fit before you push yourself on the slopes, and stretch before every downhill run. Like all adventurous sports, you must ensure that you have all the correct gear and training before you set out!

Dancing

You may have studied ballet from an early age, or you may think that's too sappy and no use at a nightclub! But whatever style of dancing you choose to do, it's an excellent way to stay fit, especially if you take regular classes. Just one night out can burn off lots of calories – just don't drink them all back again with lots of sugary cokes and other fizzy drinks!

Rock Climbing

Fear not! You're not being asked to attempt Mount Everest. Many sports centres have 'rock gyms' or indoor climbing walls where you can learn the art of rock climbing without the weather, and with less risk than on a rock face. It's great for conquering your fears – of falling or of heights – and uses nearly every muscle group in your whole body. It gives you a great buzz when you reach your target, and burns an amazing 500 or more calories each hour!

Racquet Sports

They may all seem the same, but tennis, badminton and squash all get you going at a different pace. Tennis will give you a good run around a larger court while squash will have you ducking and diving (good for your bum!). Fast and furious badminton can help you burn between 500 and 1,000 calories for every one hour's session!

Volleyball

You've seen people playing on the beach, right? Then you pretty much know the rules already. It's an easy sport to learn, and such great exercise. You can join a club to play indoors during winter. As soon as you improve, you can show off on the beach! A fab way to get fit, meet people, enjoy the sunshine AND impress the boys!

Keeping Fit – Saint or Sinner?

Don't...

✡ forget to wear a sports bra when doing exercise
✡ do any strenuous exercise without first warming up your muscles
✡ pig out on junk food after exercise – reach for a healthy snack instead

Do...

✡ at least ten minutes of strenuous activity each day
✡ find an activity that you enjoy doing, so it's fun as well as good for you
✡ be careful not to overdo it and risk injuring yourself

Playtime

You don't have to be a sport freak to keep fit!

There are lots of activities that you can do just for fun that'll tone your muscles, strengthen your body and burn off excess calories. Summer's a great time to get out in the fresh air and play, although running through puddles and having snowball fights aren't bad, either!

Winter Workout

If the weather's not so great, wrap up warm and work that body! Snowball fights are good for your arms and upper body (and your face muscles, you'll probably be laughing so much). Likewise, making an ice-slide, going sledging or skating, or building an igloo will warm you up and increase your heart rate along the way.

Child's Play

If you have younger relatives, join in with their games sometimes. You'll be amazed at how much energy they have – they'll soon leave you lagging behind! It's easy to forget how much kids run around – and did you notice they ride their bikes everywhere, just for fun! Those were the days, eh?

Beach Party

It's cool what counts as exercise if you apply a little lateral thinking. Building a sandcastle can use more than 100 calories-an-hour and provide a light workout for your arms. Playing frisbee is great for burning energy and getting your back and shoulders in shape. If you're really not that keen on sunbathing, try snorkelling (good for your legs and bum) or have an energetic game of beach volleyball (see page 25) then dive into the water to cool off afterwards.

What To Wear

It's easy to get carried away and spend a fortune on sports gear.

But it's really not worth it until you've found an activity that suits you and holds your interest for long enough. Here's a guide to what you need to bear in mind when you're getting kitted up for exercise.

Top Notch

As your body develops, you'll need to protect your boobs from too much bouncing around! It hurts, it's off-putting and it's bad for you. Buy two proper sports bras, so you can wear one while the sweaty one is being washed. You really will feel the difference!

Hair Flair

It's not a fashion statement. Wearing your hair tied back will help you play on without worrying that you can't see the ball, which way to cycle, or where your team-mates are. If your hair is too short for a ponytail, clip the front away from your eyes.

Warm Up

We don't just mean warm up your muscles! It's important to keep warm during exercise. Once you work up a sweat, your body heat will increase, but 'til then wrap up warm and comfortable.

Sweat Pants

Many trackie bottoms are made from a great fabric that actually helps to keep you cool and dry. The material transports your sweat (your body's natural cooling system) to the surface of the fabric so it can evaporate quickly. Clever, huh?

Typecast Trainers

Although lots of sports kit is general, it's advisable to get the right type of trainers for your chosen sport. Different training shoes offer support to different areas of your foot and ankle. Ask for advice at a specialist sports store before you splash your cash.

Work That Body!

What's your fave bit of your bod? Which bit, if any, needs the most attention to get into shape?

Many areas of your body can be kept in shape by targeting them with specific exercises, or by choosing the right activity from pages 22–26. Here's a cheat's guide to exercises you can do at home as well.

Workout Rules

1

Soft Surfaces
Be sure to use a mat, rug or soft carpet for floor exercises, so as not to hurt your boobs or tummy.

2

Emphasize your Breathing
Breathe in deeply before the main move and out with the main effort.

3

Don't Bounce
Slowly move your body into position, stretching further with each move.

Calves
While you're watching TV, tone up your lower legs. Sit on the edge of the sofa and straighten one leg in front of you. Keep your heel on the floor, toes pointing up. Lean your body forward to feel the stretch down the back of your leg. Hold this stretch for 20 seconds then repeat on the other leg. Do three sets altogether.

Tummy
Your tum may need some serious work as it shows wobbles easily and contains muscles that you probably don't use every day. Try this exercise while you're waiting for the bath to run. Lie on your back and raise your head and shoulders off the floor. Lift your legs up to a 45° angle and start moving them as if you're cycling. Cycle forward ten times, then change direction, cycling backwards ten times. Rest and then repeat three times.

Thighs and Bum

Next time you're on the phone, try this. Stand with your feet shoulder-width apart, toes pointing out. Bend at the knees until your thighs are almost horizontal. Don't overstretch – work up to it gradually. Keep your back straight and your tummy tucked in. Stand up straight, clenching your bum cheeks as you go. Aim for 15 repetitions each phone call. If you swing your arms vigorously (alternating which one you use to hold the phone) then you'll give them a good workout as well.

Boobs and Chest

You don't have any muscles in your boobs, so you can't make them bigger or firmer. However, you can exercise the muscles that support them to keep them looking perky. Lie on your back with your feet on the floor, knees bent. Hold a weight in each hand, palms upwards (try using bottles or tins that both weigh the same). Position your hands level with your shoulders and push up to the ceiling using your chest muscles. Lower and repeat 12 times. Do this three times.

Arms

Try this while you're waiting for the kettle to boil, or the microwave to ping. Place your hands on the kitchen worktop, a little more than shoulder-width apart. Walk your feet back a few steps until you're in a 'standing up press-ups' position. Lift onto your toes, and bend your elbows to lower your chest to the counter. Press up again and repeat 25 times. Tennis is also great exercise for your arms – see page 25 for more information on racquet sports, which will improve your arm muscles.

Fit Or Not?

Follow this fun flow chart to find out what kind of a fitness gal you really are!

catching up on the goss

head outside

sit and chill

During school breaks, I like to...

When I'm angry, I tend to...

One of my main hobbies is...

watching TV

keep it all inside until I burst

playing on the computer

I can't stand it when...

it's too hot and saps your energy

My best friends think I'm...

it rains and I'm stuck indoors

lovely just the way I am

a good listener

When I'm with my family...

mad and unpredictable

I can't wait to be with my friends

Couch Potato

Oh dear, oh dear. You seem to do a lot of talking, TV-watching and relaxing. Something's going to have to change or you may end up lazy and overweight. Why not find a gym that lets you watch TV while you jog? A fair compromise!

Runner Bean

You're full of energy! You probably lead enough of a hectic lifestyle to keep you active, but you might try channelling some of that enthusiasm into a sport. It might help you learn to concentrate and focus a little bit more.

Start

On a night out, my fave thing is...

dancing all night

During sports lessons, I'm picked early because...

I'm really good

I'm really popular

join all the clubs

Saturdays are great for...

When I'm on holiday, I...

take it out on those around me

going to netball/ judo/soccer

going shopping

catching up on watching soaps

try all the sports available

I use my mobile most for...

we love sitting and talking a lot

phoning home for a lift

texting my friends

Peas in a Pod
Life's just one big party, and you're happiest with a gang of fun friends. But think how good it would be to get all your friends together and start your own team. Burn off some energy, whilst working your body with your pals!

Keeny Beanie
You probably sussed already that you like sports! It's great that you're so fit and healthy, but make sure you spend time with friends, too. Get them in on the act, play frisbee in the park or grab some rollerblades. Sporty *and* sociable!

Looking Good

Nailed

It's all very well for models and actresses – they have perfect nails because they're surrounded by beauty therapists, right?

True – but that's why you need to get wise to the secret of beautiful, hassle-free nails that you can create yourself!

Banish Polish

If you want low-maintenance nails, avoid painting them, especially in bright colours. The first chip will make your hand look ragged. Nails also look nicer if they're all the same short to medium length.

Special Occasion?

If you want to jazz up your nails for a special night out, try the weekly workout before you do, so your nails are in tiptop condition before you apply the polish.

Long and Short of It

Make sure they're all the same length. If you break one, file the others to a medium length to better disguise the broken ones.

Don't do It!

What are the worst things you can do to your nails? Avoid these real no-nos.

1 Don't bite your nails, the skin around them, or – ouch – your cuticles.

2 Don't file them with a metal file. Always use an emery board instead, which won't chip them.

3 Don't soak them in water for too long. This can weaken them.

Weekly Workout

Take time to massage a little oil into your nails and cuticles to keep them strong. Even olive oil will do the trick! Then use a wooden emery board to smooth and shape the edges of your nails. At the same time, lightly file the ends of your nails just underneath the tips. You don't need to shorten them – it's the equivalent of having your hair trimmed to avoid split ends.

Hair Flair

If you hadn't figured it out already, a healthy lifestyle means a healthy body – and that includes your hair.

If your diet is lacking in nutrients, your hair will become dry, brittle, dull or lifeless. So the first step towards healthy hair, is to get smart with your eating habits. However, there are other remedies for bad hair days.

Do... have a trim every four to eight weeks to avoid split ends.

Greasy Hair

If you're stuck with limp or greasy hair and no time to wash, the old tricks are the best. It just needs a sprinkling of talcum powder! Brush it through to soak up some of the oils to make your hair less likely to stick to your head.

Salon Savvy

To keep your hair looking fab.

1 Protect your hair from the sun just like you protect your skin – see page 36 for more info.

2 Don't overstyle your hair. Let your hair dry naturally when you can. Pull it into a ponytail if you don't like it unstyled.

ASK FOR... HELP!

Control Those Wispies!

If you have a posh 'up do', squirt some hairspray onto an old toothbrush and ask a friend to use it to smooth into place any loose wispy ends (especially those at the back of your neck).

Quick Spritz

To liven up limp hair, tip it upside-down and spray a mist of hairspray underneath. Give it a quick brush for 'oomph' to last the day.

Tangles? Hair today... gone tomorrow!

Super Styling

After washing your hair, squeeze out any excess water and wrap a towel, turban-style, around it for ten minutes before using a wide-tooth comb to detangle it. Leave it a while longer before blowdrying it into place, as nearly-dry hair styles more easily.

Don't... scrub your hair with a towel as it damages the hair and causes split ends.

Little by Little

Don't blowdry too much hair at once. Clip some of it up and dry sections at a time, working from underneath. Don't blast your hair with the hottest setting – keep it cooler, and smooth your hair down as you go. Work your way through it, a section at a time. Finish the style off with a blast of cold air from your dryer.

BEFORE

Top Tips

For fuzz-free styles, invest in some smoothing serum. The secret to success is the way you apply it. Rub a few drops between your hands, but then use a clean blusher brush to sweep the serum off your hands and down through the ends of your hair. Alternatively, spray a tiny amount of hairspray onto the bristles of your brush and smooth it over your hair.

AFTER

Fun In The Sun

Whether you're heading to the Canary Islands, or relaxing in your back garden, you need to be sun-smart.

Even a cloudy day can leave you with a pink nose, dehydration, a sensitive scalp or – horror of horrors – white marks where your shoulder straps were! So here's everything you need to know to play it safe and cool.

Sun Spots

The sun's at its hottest in the middle of the day, so make sure you stay covered up with a hat, shades and sleeves from noon until at least 2 p.m. It's the perfect excuse to stay under your beach brolly reading a book, or lounge around having lunch and watching the world go by from the comfort of a cool café.

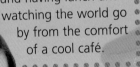

Hair Care

The best protection for your hair is a scarf or a hat, but if you don't want to wear one, spray some dry oil (sun lotion) onto your parting (to protect your scalp) and smooth a blob of conditioner through your hair before you start to sunbathe.

Pile on the Slap

Not your make-up this time – suntan lotion. Check that your lotion protects against UVA and UVB rays. UVA rays cause wrinkles, UVB cause sunburn (remember UVA for Ageing and UVB for Burn). Most long-term damage is done to your skin before you're 18, so act now. Choose an SPF (sun protection factor) of at least 10 if you're dark skinned, and 15 to 30 if you have medium to fair skin and burn easily.

In The Clear

AAAAAGH! The mere thought of spots can keep you locked in your bedroom for days, right?

Unfortunately, there's no quick-fix for the bumpy beastlies, but there are a few things you can do to help keep them at bay…

Don't… pick or squeeze spots – it will only make them worse and more noticeable!

What Spot?
Blocked pores (known as blackheads) are common on your nose and chin. Red spots may be infected blackheads, but could also be acne. Acne is clusters of raised spots, often like boils.

Always remove your make-up at night using a facewash or cleansing product, which is suited to your skin.

Do… drink lots of water, eat healthily and exercise often to improve your complexion.

And if all else Fails…
If you think you have acne, ask to see your family doctor, who can prescribe treatments that you just can't buy at the chemist. The hormone changes that occur in your teens are a major cause of acne, and it's a common skin complaint. You'll most likely grow out of it.

Use a mild, medicated facewash twice a day to keep your face super-clean.

Dress To Impress!

What shape is your body? Do you have newfound boobs, or short legs and a long body, or skinny ankles and bony arms?

Whatever your shape, there are some great clothes in the shops that will suit you perfectly and make the most of it!

Mix 'n' Match

If your exact body shape doesn't appear on this page, don't worry – you're not abnormal! Just take the right elements from these girls to create your own body shape and go with the advice for each. You'll be stylish in no time!

Vicky

✫ **Big boobs** – avoid chunky jumpers and high-necked tops. Choose open necks or tops that go in at the waist but aren't too tight on your boobs.

✫ **Muscly, well-defined arms** – show them off with tiny sleeves or vest tops.

✫ **Wide hips** – move attention to your (hopefully) slimmer waist and tummy by wearing short tops.

✫ **Short legs** – go for hipster jeans with flares or bootleg bottoms, and avoid cropped trousers.

✫ **Thick ankles** – avoid cropped trousers and choose longer-length legs.

Amy

✫ **Medium boobs** – choose flattering V-shaped necks and skinny-rib jumpers.

✫ **Chunky arms** – choose floaty blouses with sleeves that flare towards your hands and draw attention away from the tops of your arms. Also avoid tops with tiny straps, or with puff sleeves.

✫ **Big bottom** – choose jeans with pocket detail on the back to break up the width of your bum.

✫ **Long legs** – lucky girls can get away with cropped or turned-up trousers. If choosing long trousers, go for ones that reach the bottom of your heel.

Zoë

✤ **Little boobs** – make the most of being able to wear halter-necks or backless tops that you don't need to wear a bra with. Don't wear really low necklines, which only emphasize your chest.

✤ **Skinny arms** – wear chunky bracelets that draw attention to your wrists and away from the tops of your arms.

✤ **Big bottom** – wear funky hipster trousers that aren't too tight or baggy. Combats that fit well on the waist should do the trick. They draw the eye away from the size of your bum!

Katie

✤ **Little boobs** – wear fab, chunky jumpers with big rollnecks.

✤ **Chunky arms** – don't wear sleeves that stop on the widest part of your arm. Choose three-quarter length sleeves, or long flarey ones.

✤ **Short legs** – wear skirts that sit just below your knee, to show off more of your lower leg.

✤ **Big thighs** – avoid bias cut, clingy skirts and choose A-line ones.

✤ **Chunky calfs** – don't avoid skirts! A-line, knee-length skirts are flattering to your legs.

Looking Good – Saint or Sinner?

Don't...

✤ pile on the make-up, which can trap dirt in your skin and cause spots
✤ let your skin get burnt by the sun – it looks dreadful and can cause horrible long-term effects
✤ forget your feet and teeth – they both need care and attention, too

Do...

✤ eat a healthy diet, which promotes a clear complexion, shiny hair and all-round better looks!
✤ make sure you protect your skin and hair from the sun
✤ give your feet and nails some tender loving care at least once a week

Teeth And Feet

Good teeth and healthy feet can help you look like an all-round pampered and presentable girl!

The state of your mouth can say a lot about your general health. Brushing your teeth regularly is vital to prevent decay and bad breath. Wearing trendy shoes can play havoc with your feet, so treat them nicely as well.

Inside Information

1 Around three-quarters of teenagers suffer from bleeding gums, which is a sign of bad health.

2 A pale or white tongue may indicate that your diet is lacking in vital vitamins. It's that old healthy eating thing again!

3 Mouth ulcers can be a sign that you're run down. Your diet may be lacking or you could be overdoing things and need more sleep.

Clean Up

Be sure to give your tongue a scrub too sometimes. Make sure you also floss regularly to prevent the build up of plaque and gum disease.

Poo-ee!

If you suffer from bad breath it's best to get to the root of the problem rather than covering it up with gum and mouthwash. If you eat smelly foods, such as garlic and curries, try cutting them out for a while to see if the problem goes away.

Death Breath

Smoking is a sure-fire way to get stinky breath. It reduces the flow of saliva in your mouth, which makes your breath smell bad. This also happens if you don't eat. Both are bad for your health in general, so be smart and smell nicer!

Pong Alert

To avoid whiffy feet, wear sandals in the summer and socks inside your trainers. Sprinkle some bicarbonate of soda inside your trainers to soak up the sweat.

Tough Tootsies

If you have hard, dry skin on your feet, you need to invest in a pumice stone or similar. Simply rub gently at the hard patches, on dry feet, and then massage in lots of hand cream or body moisturiser.

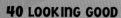

Sweet Dreams

Sleep is fantastic and bed is one of the very best places in the world – FACT!

Teenagers need between eight-and-a-half and ten hours sleep every night to look and perform their best. Sleep is the time your body needs to rejuvenate – your skin, your hair, your muscles and your brain all benefit greatly from sleep.

Sleep Cycles

To get the best from your night's sleep stick to a routine bedtime and waking time. If you need to wake at 7.00 a.m., aim to be in bed by 10.30 p.m. at the latest – more like 9.30 p.m. if you ever get snoozy during the day. Try to keep to this as much as possible at weekends.

Pillow Talk

If your problem is getting to sleep, try to wind down before bedtime. No more studying 'til the small hours, or playing computer games in bed. Soak in the bath, watch some TV or listen to music. Be sure to turn the TV off before you fall asleep as the flickering disrupts proper, restful sleep.

Snoozy Secrets

Some people believe that the way you lie in bed can reveal your personality type, and the things you dream about give clues about what's going on in your head. Try the quiz on page 42 for a fun insight into your sleeping mind!

Hey, Sleepyhead!

If you struggle to wake up in the mornings, try these to kick start your system.

1 Sing along to your radio or talk to yourself. Conversation, even with no one, gets your brain into wake-up mode.

2 Sleep with the curtains open, or get up and go into a bright room. Daylight tells your brain it's supposed to be awake.

3 Lift your knees to your chest a few times. Even small muscle movements help your brain fight off lethargy.

Take The Sleep Test!

If you're a keen believer in sleep theories, try this test to find out what your sleep positions and dreams reveal about you.

Bear in mind this is only a little fun! These theories haven't been completely proven. Many pyschologists and analysts might argue there is definite potential in the results they show, but you should take it as a light-hearted game and not too literally!

A Sleep Positions

Which way do you usually sleep?

+1. Curled up ⟳
2. Spread-eagled (on your back, arms stretched out either side of you)
3. Flat on your back
4. On your side, arms down
5. On your front
6. Sideways, arms high

B Last Thoughts

Just before bedtime write down the answers to these questions.

1. What was the last TV programme you watched?
2. What did you worry about most during the day?
3. List three things or people you've thought about today.
4. Who did you speak to most today?

C Wakey, Wakey!

Before you do anything in the morning, answer these questions about your dreams.

1. **Did you see any colours in your dream? Tick any two colours from this selection:**

   ● ● ● ○
   ○✓ ● ○✓ ○

2. **Were there any numbers in your dream? Which one(s)?**

3. **Did any of these feature? Tick the one that featured the most.**
   ☐ Air   ☐ Fire   ☐ Water

4. **Were any of these happening to you in your dream?**
   ✵ Climbing
   ✵ Falling
   ✵ Getting lost ✓
   ✵ Being chased
   ✵ Getting attacked ✓
   ✵ Being late

5. **Were you travelling in your dream? If so, how?**
   ✵ Walking
   ✵ Cycling
   ✵ Driving in a car
   ✵ Sailing
   ✵ Flying
   ✵ On the bus

Analyse This!

Your sleep secrets can now be revealed with the answers to the quiz!

A Sleep Positions

1. Shows shyness, and inner sensitivity.
2. You dislike being centre of attention, but like socializing and are a good listener.
3. You're probably a perfectionist, quiet and reserved.
4. A relaxed person who gets on well in a group of people.
5. Outgoing and often loud, your confidence may be masking nerves and insecurities.
6. Ooh, dear – you're suspicious and hyper-critical, often cynical about others.

B Last Thoughts

Did anything that happened during the day feature in your dreams?

C Wakey, Wakey!

1. Colours
Red is a sign of love or anger.
Orange signifies confidence or lack of it.
Dark blue shows you're feeling blue. Light blues are optimistic.
Pink is full of optimism and happiness.
Black means you're letting things get to you.
White is promising. You may figure out the answer to a problem or face new things.
Yellow signifies light, sunshine or laughter.
Green dreams are about healing.

2. Numbers
1 All about you.
2 Your life feels slightly imbalanced.
3 Get arty and creative.
4 Suggests you have hard work ahead.
5 Go for adventure!
6 If linked to a person, this shows honesty.
7 Time to stop dallying and get going.
8 Brings luck to those who work hard.
9 Kindness – hopefully from you to help someone who needs some TLC.
10 Something is going perfectly!

3. Elements
Air shows opportunities and freedom.
Fire indicates strong feelings or security.
Water echoes your waking life, be it rough and stormy, or calm and serene.

4. Events
Climbing shows you're ambitious.
Falling shows fears or hang-ups.
Getting lost signifies loneliness, or being unsettled with close ones.
Being chased shows worries you won't face.
Getting attacked is a sign of things coming to a head, such as an argument.
Being late shows you fear to let people down.

5. Travelling
Walking shows you're an independent gal!
Cycling indicates that you're getting closer to one of your goals.
Driving in a car shows you feel in control and know where you're heading in life.
Sailing indicates an emotional journey – was it rough, or plain-sailing?
Flying shows high-flying ambition.
On the bus means don't miss opportunites!

Growing UP

Sam
8737 938

by Katie
Age 3

Standing Solo

You've reached an age when you want to stand on your own two feet. Cool, right?

But also maybe a bit scary sometimes? The thing to remember in life is that everyone – yep, everyone from the prime minister to the manager of your favourite football team – gets scared sometimes. The thing is, everyone has had to learn how to get on with stuff and not let fear get in their way, and you can learn that, too.

Leave Me Alone

Part of doing stuff on your own is being confident enough to try in the first place. There's more about confidence on page 47. However, a big step you have to make is being responsible enough to act like an independent person, without grown-ups getting you down by distrusting you.

Gaining Trust

There's an easy way and a hard way to gain people's trust. The easy way is to show you're mature enough to be trusted and left to get on with it. The hard way is to act like a little kid in a teenager's body – you know, sulking, yelling, crying or getting angry if you don't get your own way. Take a step back and look at the two approaches. Which would any normal person choose? Would you trust someone who was making a scene, or would you rather go with the calm, sensible, mature person? Well?

ASK FOR... HELP!

Heart to Heart

Take the time to sit and talk properly with your parents or guardians. Ask them if they think you're grown-up enough to do your own stuff now. If not, ask them why not, then you can work on improving the points that are holding you back. Find out what they're most scared about for you, so you can put their mind at rest. Be upfront about these things and they shouldn't turn into problems.

Be In Control

It doesn't have to be all shouting, disagreements and sulking.

There is an easier way, honest! All you have to do is compromise a little!

Getting Along

Although you didn't choose your own set of grown-ups, they chose you. So they do probably quite like you, and want you to be happy! Make the most of this, and let them know, in a calm and mature way, what you'd really like to do with your time. Be prepared to compromise. Although they want you to be happy, they're not likely to agree to you going to all-night parties during the week, or leaving school at the age of 13 to join the circus!

Getting Along Rules

1 Involve the Grown-ups
If they know what you're up to, they're more likely to leave you to it.

2 Tit for Tat
If you do some of their stuff, they might let you do your own stuff, too.

3 Make Promises
An "I'll be back by nine" will show them you're thinking of them.

4 Keep your Promises
Show up when you said you would and their belief in you will grow.

Give and Take

Don't worry, the lecture's nearly over! There's just one more thing. Having said that your grown-ups chose you, don't you think you owe them just a little time in return for the decade and a bit they've devoted to you so far? Grown-ups are actually quite easily pleased – just talk to them at the meal table and spend some quality time doing family stuff, and you'll have them just where you want them!

Think Positive

Now, here's an issue that covers life's tiniest aspects and your biggest decisions.

Confidence (and lack of it) can make or break a situation. A huge step to feeling confident is thinking good things about yourself. This has great knock-on effects. It makes you more attractive, it helps you overcome most problems and it makes you much less of a target for bullies.

Some Reasons to be Cheerful

- You've just got your braces off and have beautiful teeth.
- Your mum is sooooo cool!
- It's summer and there's a week 'til term ends. Hurray!
- Your best pal's coming for a sleepover.
- You've gone a whole week without little bro getting on your nerves.
- You've chosen to wear just the right top today to compliment your eyes.
- You've just finished all your exams.
- You've rediscovered some old jeans in your wardrobe that fit fabulously.
- You got picked for the school team and have a match on Saturday.
- Your big sis has said you can have her clothes that don't fit any more.
- Your bedroom has a great view of the park and you can see squirrels out there.
- You're going to curl up later with your brand new book.

Things to Remember

1 Speak Up

If you're in a group, it's easier to talk if you make your mark early, speak clearly and look at people directly.

2 See Through It

Someone who's loud could be trying to make up for a lack of confidence. Don't let them push you out.

3 Try Something New

Experience builds confidence and makes you better-equipped to face any situation.

Morning Motivation

Every day, sit in front of the mirror and find three things to be positive about.

- One thing that you like about yourself.
- One thing that makes you happy.
- One thing that you're really lucky to have in your life, perhaps a friend or a pet!

Feeling Uneasy?

If you feel unsure in any situation, ask someone you trust for help. You don't have to battle through everything on your own. Even better, sometimes you might find they feel the exact same way, and you can join forces to beat the problem!

Feeling Hormonal?

Yikes! It's the word that strikes fear into the hearts of Mums and Dads everywhere!

Their little girl has got some hormones and could turn into a monster at any minute! But what exactly does happen to you during puberty?

The Science

As you mature, your body changes from the body of a girl to the body of a woman. Hormones are chemical 'messengers' that make this happen. There are two main hormones responsible – oestrogen and testosterone (although the testosterone hormone is more dominant in males than females). During puberty, increased levels of hormones cause your breasts to grow, pubic hair to appear, and your periods to start (see pages 52–53).

The Crazy Statistics

Just to make you smile if the science is getting you down…

1 There are more than two million sweat glands in the human body.

2 The fastest-growing human hair is beard hair, which could grow an average of over 9 m long if never shaved or trimmed in a lifetime.

3 About 30 times more sweat can be held in a hairy armpit than a hairless one. Eugh!

The Bad News

One of the effects of your increased oestrogen levels is powerful emotional changes. These often take the form of PMT (pre-menstrual tension) which can trigger mood swings. That, plus period pains, can make you monstrous each month. See page 53 for more information on periods.

The Good News

Boys have more testosterone than girls and it can often cause spots. So take pity on your poor male school mate whose skin has just erupted!

Getting Emotional

A lot of your changing emotions can be blamed on your hormones, but not all of them.

Surveys have found that teenagers worry – a lot. And about a lot of things.

> Don't...
> bottle things up as this can make you miserable and even unwell.

Look At Me

Around half of teenage girls say they don't like their appearance. Your body is throwing new problems at you – wearing a bra, finding clothes that flatter your body shape, making the best of greasy hair when your period's due. Coping with these things can cause stress.

Lean On Me

Talking about your problems often makes them seem a lot smaller. Choose your fave grown-up to confide in. Or phone Childline free on 0800 1111 if you don't know who to talk to.

ASK FOR... HELP!

> Do...
> share your problems – perhaps with a friend, a grown-up or a sibling.

Family Values

Your home life is supposed to be a safe haven, but for many young people it's full of conflict. You may hear your parents arguing and worry about them splitting up. Even if divorce isn't on the cards, families often have blazing rows as children get older and more independent. None of it's nice to live with.

Term Time

More than 80% of teenagers say they worry so much about exams that they can't sleep properly. Add to that the proportion who don't like their teacher, or their school, or are being bullied, and that's a heap of stress and worry.

Hey, Girlfriend!

Eek! It's that time in your life when you might start fancying boys and even dating!

The good news is, you're not alone. Many of your mates will be considering the same steps. The bad news is, even grown-ups can find relationships difficult to manage, so there isn't a list of ten things guaranteed to make them work.

Let's Talk about Sex

There are too many issues surrounding this topic to cover them all on a page. In the UK, it is illegal for girls under the age of 16 to have sex, so don't let anyone try to make you sleep with them if you're too young. Add to that the precautions you must take to prevent catching sexually-transmitted diseases (STDs) or getting pregnant and you should think very hard before you have sex.

Breaking the Ice

If you've got your eye on someone, but don't really know them, what can you do? The answer is simple – talk to them. You don't have to be pushy, or risk feeling silly. Just wait 'til the next time you're near them and see if they look in your direction. If they do, just say "hi" and see what happens! Chances are, they might be feeling scared and shy too, but if they say "hi" back, it's a good start.

Fancy Free

If you try to break the ice with someone and they laugh or make nasty comments, don't be put off. They could be trying to cover up their own shyness. Try again when they're on their own. If they're rude again, it's probably best to find someone else.

There's so much choice out there, chances are you'll meet people who just don't fancy you. It's no big deal – think of all the people you just don't like in that way.

Seek Advice!

If you're finding it hard to chat to boys, ask your friends how they do it. They might have some tips to build your confidence. But be sure to choose which advice you follow. It has to feel right for you.

Starting Out

In any relationship – whether a boyfriend, best pal, schoolmate or a family member – it is important to be fair and honest about who you are. There's no point pretending to like football if it actually bores you silly. It's far better to spend your time with people who like the stuff you do.

Peer Pressure

Don't be cajoled into doing things just because your friends start doing them. It shouldn't be about keeping up – it's about what's right for you, and when you feel happy to make such important decisions.

Confide in Me

Be careful who you trust to share your secrets with. It could be round your school in minutes – how embarrassing! If this happens, just hold your head high and laugh it off. After all, everyone has secrets. It'll all be forgotten in a day or two!

It's that 'Birds and Bees' Talk!

It's best to talk to a grown-up about all the issues surrounding sex. Pick a quiet time for a one-to-one chat. Lots of grown-ups feel awkward talking to teenagers about sex – they're not sure whether to talk about the science of sex, or tackle the emotional aspects. Ask them questions about the subject to make it easier for them to talk about the stuff you really want to know.

Body Changes

You're probably noticing lots of changes to your body right now.

If you've read page 48 then you'll have some idea why they're happening. But what exactly does your body think it's playing at?!

Boobs 'r' Us

All girls have boobs in case they decide to have babies one day. However, there's a variation in the size and shape of female breasts. Breasts start to grow as puberty strikes, between the ages of nine and 19, but there's no rule about how much they'll grow. All boobs need a bra to give them support and stop the surrounding tissue from stretching. And you might as well face it – boys are always going to notice them.

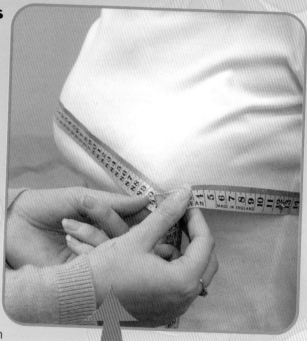

Other Changes

You'll also notice your body becoming hairier during puberty. Many girls choose to shave their armpits and legs, especially in the summer, to help reduce odour or because they think it looks nicer. However, be aware that once you've shaved body hair, it grows back as stubble, which is much less fine and downy, so you'll need to keep shaving from then on. Never shave the hair on your forearms as scratchy, stubbly arms aren't too nice.

Measuring Up

When you first develop breasts, you should invest in a decent bra. You can go to a store where they'll measure you and tell you which size to wear. Or if you're too shy to do this, ask a friend or family member to do it for you instead. Measure the distance around your torso just under your breasts to get the chest size, then on top of them to calculate what cup size you need.

Boys and Boobs

Now you're going to have to rise above any childishness from the opposite sex. If they make personal comments be the better sex and walk on by with your head held high...

A Month In The Life...

... of you, a girl who has periods.

Here's what to expect from the 28-day cycle that is (boo!) menstruation.

Days 1–7
Period time – if you're one of the unlucky ones who gets aches and cramps, then gentle exercise can help. Use tampons or sanitary towels to keep you fresh and clean.

Days 8–14
Your period should have finished. Other than a few spots from the hormone surges you were having, it's all good!

Days 15–21
Time to forget that periods even exist.

Days 22–28
If you suffer from pre-menstrual tension (PMT) then get ready for mood-swings and tiredness. Some women get tender boobs, nausea, and stomach cramps about now! Take comfort in the fact it won't last long!

ASK FOR...

Menstrual Melancholy
If your periods really get you down, talk to a grown-up. They may just be a good shoulder to cry on, or they may suggest you visit the doctor to get help overcoming them.

Period Pointers

1 Choose carefully between towels or tampons. Read the packets to decide.

2 It is vital to change a towel or tampon as suggested on the pack. They get uncomfortable if you don't!

3 Always carry some sanitary items with you. You may not always be aware of when you're about to start and you don't want to be caught out!

Growing Up – Saint or Sinner?

Don't...
✿ sulk, yell or argue in an attempt to get your own way – it's just childish and will make you look silly
✿ keep problems to yourself – talk to someone you can trust about them
✿ be pushed into things that you're not comfortable about

Do...
✿ discuss things in a calm and logical way, and remain rational
✿ think positive things about yourself and the things in your life
✿ always be yourself and never pretend to be someone you're not

Boys, Boys, Boys!

What kind of guy is your Mr Right?

Follow the pink arrows for True and the orange arrows for False.

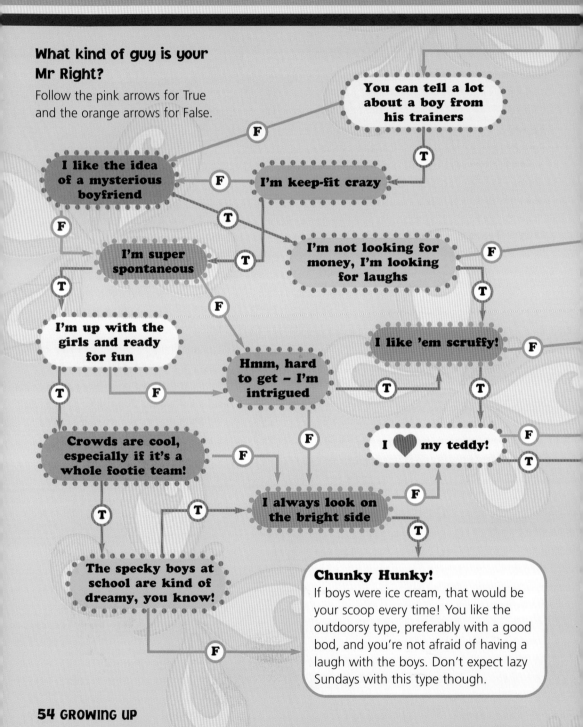

You can tell a lot about a boy from his trainers

I like the idea of a mysterious boyfriend

I'm keep-fit crazy

I'm super spontaneous

I'm not looking for money, I'm looking for laughs

I'm up with the girls and ready for fun

Hmm, hard to get – I'm intrigued

I like 'em scruffy!

Crowds are cool, especially if it's a whole footie team!

I ♥ my teddy!

I always look on the bright side

The specky boys at school are kind of dreamy, you know!

Chunky Hunky!
If boys were ice cream, that would be your scoop every time! You like the outdoorsy type, preferably with a good bod, and you're not afraid of having a laugh with the boys. Don't expect lazy Sundays with this type though.

Start

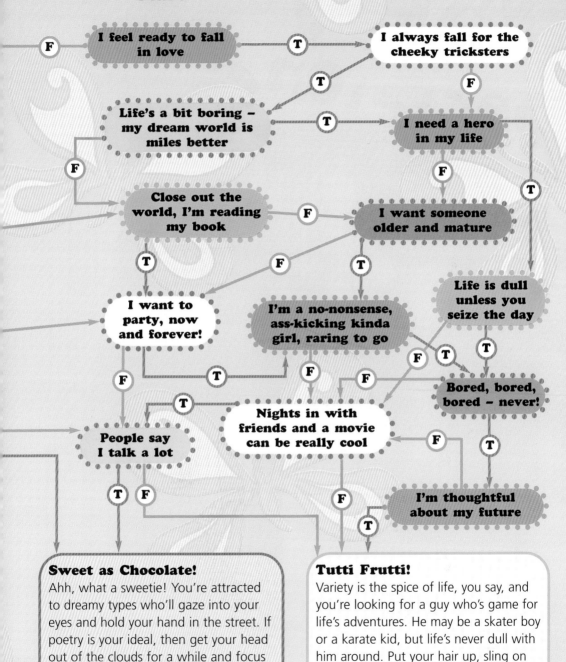

I feel ready to fall in love — F / T

I always fall for the cheeky tricksters — T / F

Life's a bit boring – my dream world is miles better — T / F

I need a hero in my life — T / F

Close out the world, I'm reading my book — F / T

I want someone older and mature — F / T

Life is dull unless you seize the day — T

I want to party, now and forever! — F / T

I'm a no-nonsense, ass-kicking kinda girl, raring to go — F / F / T

Bored, bored, bored – never! — F / T

People say I talk a lot — T / F / T

Nights in with friends and a movie can be really cool — F / F

I'm thoughtful about my future — T

Sweet as Chocolate!
Ahh, what a sweetie! You're attracted to dreamy types who'll gaze into your eyes and hold your hand in the street. If poetry is your ideal, then get your head out of the clouds for a while and focus on the reality of fancying someone!

Tutti Frutti!
Variety is the spice of life, you say, and you're looking for a guy who's game for life's adventures. He may be a skater boy or a karate kid, but life's never dull with him around. Put your hair up, sling on your running shoes and join the fun!

Making Decisions

Swallow
Health Spa

Gemma

How can I help?

**College
of Arts**

**Student
ID Card**

No: 786704

Name: Gemma Holme
Form: 2A

Make Yourself Heard!

Now you're officially getting grown-up, it's time to stand up for your rights.

You should be noticing by now that people listen to what you have to say, on many different subjects. Welcome to the adult world of having an opinion and being able to change things about your life.

Worthy Causes

People have strong feelings about many things. Often it's the environment, politics, animal rights or local youth issues. You might feel that you can't make a difference – but you can, if you approach it properly.

Not Seeing Eye to Eye

Beware of getting into heated discussions. Some issues can cause bad feelings. Before you debate with your Dad, or big sis, try a similar discussion with an objective adult, such as a teacher. It's a good way to see how other people feel about your pet subject. However, be prepared for others to not see things as you do.

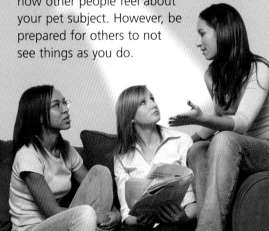

Actions Speak Loudest

If just talking is wearing thin, and you want to feel like you're making a real difference, there are many organized groups who try to do just that. Ask your library about local environment or animal rights groups, or contact your local MPs to see if they have youth groups that you can join.

Emotional Issues

To make your voice heard, it's vital to be prepared. Before you start arguing your point with others, answer these questions.

1 Do you know lots of facts about your chosen subject?

2 Can you present the facts in a logical argument?

3 Are you aware of the arguments against your own views?

4 Can you put forward your point without getting over-emotional?

Going Global

Look online for like-minded people. All the major UK political parties have youth wings, and international organizations, such as Greenpeace and WWF, are always looking for new members. This is a great way to make a difference, and to increase your knowledge of your chosen topic.

Health And Safety

Is it illegal to drink alcohol or take drugs? What happens if you try them?

The chances are you may be going out more and you may meet people who offer you drink or drugs. What should you do?

Rules and Regs

The laws in the UK are there to protect young people from things that are bad for them. It's illegal to buy or drink alcohol (except in your home) under the age of 18, although restaurants can serve you from 16. Drugs are treated differently – it's illegal to have them at all. There are some exceptions for things your doctor could prescribe.

What's so Bad?

Regardless of the law, it's sensible to avoid drugs completely, and to be very careful with alcohol. Drinking or taking drugs can badly affect your physical development, health and safety. They can damage internal organs, such as your liver and kidneys, and have a bad effect on your brain. They can also change the way you behave, and lead to you doing things you don't want to do.

Substance Abuse

Substance abuse is the term for doing drugs, smoking cigarettes and drinking alcohol. It covers situations where you're using an external source that can harm your body. What exactly can it do to you? See the table below for the shocking facts.

Substance	Short-term Effects	Long-term Effects	Fatal Effects
Alcohol	hangovers; bad breath; loss of judgement; injury from clumsiness; risk of humiliation	liver damage; arthritis; depression; insomnia; damage to all major internal organs	alcohol poisoning can cause instant death; fatal risk-taking as a result of impaired safety awareness
Cigarettes	bad cough; bad breath; yellow fingers, nails and teeth; addiction	heart disease; stroke; stomach ulcers; bronchitis; raised blood pressure; cancer; emphysema	cancer can kill; chance of fatal stroke
Inhalants (i.e. glue)	mood swings; headache; hallucinations; dizziness; stomach pain	nausea; nosebleeds; brain damage; incontinence; violent behaviour; damage to liver, lungs and kidneys	sudden death, often through suffocation, even on first try
Drugs	hallucinations; sleepiness; impaired memory; lack of concentration	increased cancer risk; difficulty having children; psychological damage	cancer in later life; chances of overdose that can cause instant death, or brain damage

Hangovers – Yuck!

The after-effects of drink and drugs are lousy. Just ask a grown-up what hangovers (from drinking) are like. You'll wonder why people ever get drunk at all! Think about your worst period pains, with a headache and lots of sickness... it's not something you'd volunteer for, is it?

What Drugs Contain

It's worth mentioning that many illegal drugs are made by people who think only of the money they make from them. These people do not care about your safety, and so could be putting hazardous substances into the drugs they sell. That's scary stuff!

Future Implications

Aside from all the health and safety issues, being caught taking illegal drugs can also give you a criminal record. This could cause problems in the future when you try to gain employment or travel abroad.

Staying Safe

You know about avoiding drink and drugs and the effects both can have. But there are other safety issues you should be aware of, in everyday situations. Females have to take more safety measures than males to keep themselves safe at all times. Don't stay in situations that unnerve you, such as an empty train carriage or bus. Never walk home alone after dark or in isolated spots. Too many people think it won't happen to them – but it's best not to risk it.

Don't be Scared

This information isn't meant to frighten you – it's meant to make you aware. Statistics show that people aware of their surroundings are more likely to successfully prevent or escape attack. Common sense is your best weapon. Your brain has evolved over millions of years to teach you survival instincts that should help you out of most situations.

Risk Assessment

Let's face it, you're unlikely to win a fight with someone much bigger than you. It will be better to flee than fight. You can learn some basic self-defence that could gain you a couple of minutes advantage to run away.

> Do... stand up for yourself and say "no" when you know something is wrong.

Butt Kicking

Find out about classes in women's self defence. Many attackers won't expect you to fight back, and you could gain a vital few seconds to run away and find help. You can learn some basic moves that might help you out of dangerous situations. But it is vital that you only use these when strictly necessary! Don't go getting into trouble just to test out your new moves!

Beat The Blushes

Another awful aspect of growing up is getting embarrassed.

Think of those situations you dread, such as falling over in public, mistaking a stranger for someone you know or leaving the loo with your skirt tucked in your knickers! Now think of how people cope with them – it's no big deal, is it? So what's changed?

Troubleshooting

Deal with embarrassing situations head on! Acknowledge openly when you mess up, and your humiliation will fade. The worst thing you can do is say nothing to anyone who witnessed your embarrassment and then continue to beat yourself up over it.

Top 10 Embarrassing Moments

1 Walking into the wrong classroom.

2 Wearing totally the wrong outfit for a party.

3 Being tongue-tied with a gorgeous guy.

4 Having your parents show you up – for any reason!

5 Dying your hair and it turning totally the wrong colour.

6 Farting in public (how rude!).

7 Meeting your boyfriend's parents for the first time and saying something stupid.

8 Setting off the security alarm in a shop.

9 Bitching about someone then finding them right behind you.

10 Shouting over loud music that stops as you're mid-sentence.

What about the Knickers Thing?

What's the worst that could happen? So people see your pants? Unless they're dirty or inappropriately sexy (either way, shame on you girl!) then seriously, don't worry. Everyone wears pants, don't they? And it's only like walking down the beach in your swimsuit. Don't stress so much! Everyone gets embarrassed at some point – yes, everyone! We've all been there!

ASK FOR...

Let It All Out!
If you're dying of humiliation, tell someone about it. They'll probably help you see the funny side of it, and might tell you their own stories of gut-wrenchingly horrible things that happened to them. Once you see that it happens to everyone, and they survive it, you'll be able to put it into perspective. Just as long as you didn't do anything TOO awful…!

Deal with It
Look through the Top Ten list. Which of these would be your very worst nightmare? Which of them could you avoid? Which could you prepare for? Part of your coping tactics to beat the blushes is planning ahead. In situations such as 3, 5 and 7, think through the scenario to figure out how you'd like to handle it. This will make you more confident and more relaxed, so things are much less likely to go wrong.

Don't Go There
Situations like 6 and 9 can be avoided altogether. Bitching and gossiping never do any good, so it kinda serves you right if you get caught out – and the same goes for rude noises! As for the others, you just have to rise above them. Everyone gets shown up by their parents, has a hair disaster, or makes a bad fashion choice. Save the story for a good laugh next time you're swapping cringe-tales at a sleepover.

Making Decisions – Saint or Sinner?

Don't...
✯ let a part-time job interfere with your school work
✯ experiment with drugs, alcohol or smoking – you should be able to enjoy yourself without them anyway
✯ leave your future plans and career choices entirely to chance

Do...
✯ research any careers that interest you as it's great to have a goal
✯ be strong enough to say "no" when you know something is wrong
✯ be aware of safety at all times and stay out of uncomfortable or potentially-dangerous situations

I Need Some Cash!

If you haven't got to final year exams yet, or are continuing your education, you might want part-time work.

Most students are skint – fact! There are lots of options if you want to work at weekends or even on schooldays, but there are also some legal restrictions.

It's the Law

You can't work for pay until you're 14. Then it's only a max of five hours on Saturdays, two hours on Sundays, and 25 hours a week during the school holidays. Once you're 15, you can work up to eight hours on Saturdays, two on Sundays and 35 hours a week in the holidays. Under 16s can't work during school hours, for more than 17 hours a week in term time, or between the hours of 7.00 p.m. and 7.00 a.m. The laws are there to protect you and ensure that working doesn't affect your school work.

What Can I Do?

Under 18s aren't allowed to work with alcohol, gambling, heavy machinery or dangerous substances. Many young people choose to do a paper round, or work in a shop, restaurant or hotel. Babysitting or car washing are good for extra cash. There is no minimum wage until you're 18, so don't expect to make a million straight off!

> Don't...
> let a part-time job interfere with your school work.

ASK FOR...

HELP!

Making Work Arrangements

Always ask your parents or guardians before you agree to take a job. Make sure you can get there and back safely, especially if you need to travel when it's dark.

Girl Power

Girls are better than boys, right? At least, in this day and age, they have a lot more opportunity to do the same stuff as boys.

Make the most of modern attitudes about equality to do what you want in your life. Remember, girls never used to play football, or be scientists, or make a million. Now you can do all that, plus still get to enjoy shopping and wear high-heels, too!

Girls in Lurve

It's not just the serious stuff that has changed for girls. You can now jump in the driving seat where relationships are concerned, too! There's nothing wrong with taking the lead and approaching a boy you fancy to chat him up, or ask him out. After all, why should boys always have to risk rejection?

Girls at Work

Lots of careers were once thought of as 'male only' but that's just not the case any more. Ten minutes surfing the web can give you lots of information about jobs in previously male-dominated careers, such as science or technology. Girls get better exam results than boys, so make the most of it to grab the best careers!

Girls in Politics

Around one-quarter of EU (European Union) politicians are female, and nearly one-fifth of the UK's Members of Parliament are women. These numbers have been rising steadily over the years, and politics needs women like you to help increase the proportion of women who want to make a difference to the country. It has been said that, "When women have a voice in national and international affairs, wars will cease forever." Do you care enough about your world to make such a difference?

What's Next?

As you reach the end of your school years, you're faced with the big question – what next?

There will probably be bags of careers help and advice at your school, but it's worth investigating things for yourself as well. Research your options to see what you like.

No more School!

Some people can't wait to finish their education and get a job. If that's what you want to do, don't let people push you into more studying. Prove to others that you've got some job choices in mind – ones that don't need further qualifications – then set yourself a time limit to find a job before considering other options. If you think you've made the wrong decision, there's nothing to stop you applying for higher education later on.

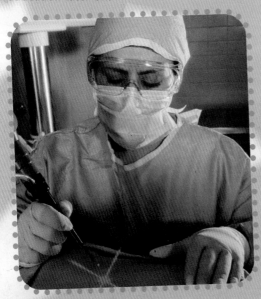

ASK FOR... HELP!

Ask Around
Ask lots, actually! The problem with careers services is that they're limited in the jobs they can describe to you. Ask everyone you meet what they do, and if it appeals to you, ask for more info to help you decide if it's for you. Most people like talking about their jobs to people who show an interest.

Lots more Learning

Some people continue their education for some years. This could be because they genuinely enjoy learning, or because they want to experience what higher education can offer. Others know that's what's needed for their chosen profession as a lawyer or doctor, for example. If you don't wish to continue education, you might be lucky enough to find that your chosen career offers an apprenticeship. This enables you to start work, get paid, AND study to get professional qualifications!

Tinker, Tailor...
What kind of job would suit you? Some things are obvious. For example, you can't be a vet if you don't like animals. But there are other things to consider. Use pages 66–67 to narrow down your choices, or read through the jobs on page 65 for ideas.

Realistic

Vet or veterinary assistant
Engineer (chemical/electrical/mechanical)
Athlete
Gardener or landscaper
Tree surgeon
Surveyor
Construction worker
Geologist
Decorator

Investigative

Teacher
Auditor
Health and safety officer
Food scientist
Financial advisor
Biologist
Clinical psychologist
Sociologist
Doctor

Conventional

Accountant
Stockbroker
Proofreader
Library technician
Auditor
Clerk (insurance/court/office)
Legal secretary
PA (personal assistant)
Administrative clerk

Social

Occupational therapist
Speech therapist
Prison officer
Social worker
Counsellor
Nurse
Funeral director
Security guard
Tour guide

Artistic

Musician (performer/composer/teacher)
Editor (words/music/film)
Writer (journalist/author/advertising)
TV/film (producer/camera operator/star)
Florist
Make-up artist
Photographer
Advertising
Designer (graphic/interior/fashion)

Enterprising

Business manager
Conference organizer
Estate agent
Law (police/solicitor/judge)
Sales person
Telemarketing
Buyer
Financial controller
Treasurer

What Work Suits You?

1 **Tick the six statements that are most like you**

- [ ] I prefer working in a group.
- [x] I'm happy to share ideas with others.
- [x] I can work with lots of noise around me.
- [x] I don't mind working on my own.
- [ ] I'm happiest working with a computer.
- [x] I'm good at following instructions.

- [x] I'm good at helping others learn.
- [ ] I think other people are as capable as me.
- [x] I enjoy solving problems and puzzles.
- [x] I get distracted easily.
- [ ] I like to work things out in my own way.
- [ ] When I start something, I like to finish it.

Count up your scores. Did you tick more statements in the blue row or the yellow row?
If you ticked mostly blue, go to box 3. If you ticked mostly yellow, go to box 2.

2 **Tick all the statements that describe you best**

- [ ] I'm quite sporty.
- [ ] I love to build and reconstruct things.
- [x] Maths is one of my fave subjects.
- [ ] Silly mistakes really frustrate me.
- [x] I love designing clothes and jewellery.
- [x] My imagination often runs away with me.

- [x] I love playing computer games.
- [ ] I don't like many subjects at school.
- [ ] I pay meticulous attention to details.
- [x] I like some routine in my life.
- [x] I love drawing and painting.
- [x] I prefer English to Maths or IT.

Did you tick mostly blue? Check out the jobs for Realistic people on page 67.
Did you tick more green? You should read all about Conventional jobs on page 67.
Were you more pink than the others? Read about Artistic jobs on page 67.

3 **Tick all the statements that describe you best**

- [x] I love solving or analysing problems.
- [ ] Science is one of my fave subjects.
- [x] I'm a good listener and like people.
- [ ] I like English and am good with words.
- [x] I'd like to make lots of money.
- [x] I'm good in a role of responsibility.

- [ ] I trust things I see rather than my instinct.
- [ ] I love learning or teaching new things.
- [ ] I don't want to do a boring desk job.
- [x] Everyone should realize their potential.
- [x] I don't mind if some people dislike me.
- [x] I have an idea of what I want out of life.

Did you tick mostly yellow? Check out the jobs for Investigative people on page 67.
Did you tick more orange? You should try a Social job, read what this is on page 67.
Were you more purple than the others? Read all about Enterprising jobs on page 67.

Realistic

You're not exactly suited to a regular desk job, are you? That means there's a whole load of other stuff out there, though – manually-skilled professionals are often in short supply. You'd love your training to be on-the-job if possible.

Conventional

You'd be great at a job working with data, or doing clerical tasks. You're probably very good with numbers, and following instructions or doing detailed work. Some people might find it boring, but you thrive on the structure and routine.

Artistic

No surprise, you'd like a job allowing you to be creative, innovative or purely artistic. You're not very good at working in a structured environment. You can be very intuitive and open-minded and may be able to use that in your career.

Investigative

You like people, but equally you like facts – delving into something until you get to the roots of the issue. You love analysing and solving problems, and enjoy being around other people who like to learn, too.

Social

Hey, people person! You don't mind what you do as long as it helps others and involves lots of personal contact. You're great at training, helping or even curing other people, and love to pass on something of benefit at every meeting.

Enterprising

You'll be tab at a job that requires you to influence other people – whether it's for financial gain or just to see a job well done. You're good at persuading, too – a natural leader, some might say.

Now, turn to page 65 for some job suggestions to suit your type. Don't be surprised if you're a mix of a couple of types – read the job lists for both and see if anything grabs you!

January

Date	What's on this week?			
1				
2				
3				
4				
5				
6				
7				

Remember! Remember!

It is essential to eat at least five portions of fruit and vegetables every day to maintain a healthy body, skin, hair and nails.

January

Date	What's on this week?
8	
9	
10	
11	
12	
13	
14	

Remember! Remember!

Do small things each day to keep fit and exercise. Take the stairs instead of a lift whenever you can or walk to a friend's house.

January

Date	What's on this week?			
15				
16				
17				
18				
19				
20				
21				

Remember! Remember!

Don't overstyle your hair. Save your straighteners for the weekend if you can, and try to let your hair dry naturally as often as possible.

January

Date	What's on this week?
22	
23	
24	
25	
26	
27	
28	

Remember!
Remember!

Always remove any make-up at night, and cleanse your face twice a day to keep your face clean and less prone to spots or blemishes.

January–February

Date	What's on this week?			
29				
30				
31				
1				
2				
3				
4				

Remember! Remember!

You need between eight-and-a-half and ten hours sleep every night in order to look and perform your best throughout the day.

February

Date	What's on this week?			
5				
6				
7				
8				
9				
10				
11				

Remember! Remember!

Try to spend time with your family. Even just chatting to them over the dinner table each night will help your relationship with them.

February

Date	What's on this week?			
12				
13				
14				
15				
16				
17				
18				

Remember! Remember!

Always be true to yourself. Don't let anyone persuade you to do things you're uncomfortable with or don't feel happy doing.

February

Date	What's on this week?			
19				
20				
21				
22				
23				
24				
25				

Remember! Remember!

Beware of getting into heated discussions with the people you live with about causes or topics that you feel passionately about.

February–March

Date	What's on this week?			
26				
27				
28				
29				
1				
2				
3				

Remember! Remember!

If you feel horribly embarrassed or humiliated about something, it's often good to talk to someone about it and get it off your chest.

March

Date	What's on this week?			
4				
5				
6				
7				
8				
9				
10				

Remember! Remember!

A good diet is all about balance. You can still have sugary treats or fatty foods as long as you balance your daily intake of these with healthier foods.

March

Date	What's on this week?			
11				
12				
13				
14				
15				
16				
17				

Remember! Remember!

Your body is like a machine. Different foods help different parts of your body. See pages 12–13 for more information.

March

Date	What's on this week?
18	
19	
20	
21	
22	
23	
24	

Remember! Remember! You should aim to drink at least eight medium glasses of water each day, to keep your body hydrated and working properly.

March

Date	What's on this week?			
25				
26				
27				
28				
29				
30				
31				

Remember! Remember!

Exercise is essential to prevent excessive weight gain. Obesity can cause all sorts of health problems. So be sure to get plenty of exercise to keep your weight stable.

April

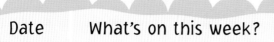

Date	What's on this week?			
1				
2				
3				
4				
5				
6				
7				

April

Date	What's on this week?			
8				
9				
10				
11				
12				
13				
14				

Remember! Remember!

It's important to wear warm and comfortable clothing during exercise. You shouldn't wear tight or restrictive items or feel cold when you start out.

April

Date	What's on this week?		
15			
16			
17			
18			
19			
20			
21			

Remember! Remember!

To keep your nails looking nice, ensure they are kept clean and tidy. Try not to paint them bright colours too often and keep them all at a similar length.

April

Date	What's on this week?			
22				
23				
24				
25				
26				
27				
28				

Remember! Remember!

When outside in the sunshine, always wear a sun lotion that protects against UVA and UVB rays and prevents your skin from burning or long-term damage.

April–May

Date	What's on this week?			
29				
30				
1				
2				
3				
4				
5				

Remember! Remember!

Different clothes suit different body shapes. Think about what your shape is and use the advice on pages 38–39 to pick outfits that make the most of your figure.

May

Date	What's on this week?			
6				
7				
8				
9				
10				
11				
12				

Remember! Remember!

If you want to get along with adults, it's important to keep promises you make, such as turning up when you said you would or completing homework on time.

May

Date	What's on this week?			
13				
14				
15				
16				
17				
18				
19				

Remember! Remember!

Puberty is the natural development of your body, from girl to woman. The appearance of pubic hair and starting of periods are all things that help you mature.

May

Date	What's on this week?			
20				
21				
22				
23				
24				
25				
26				
27				

May–June

Date	What's on this week?
28	
29	
30	
31	
1	
2	
3	

Remember! Remember!

Never pretend to be something you're not. You should always be open and honest about who you are and not try to impress people with alternative personalities.

June

Date	What's on this week?			
4				
5				
6				
7				
8				
9				
10				

Remember! Remember!

Always carry some sanitary items with you. You might not always know when your period is due and you don't want to be caught out.

June

Date	What's on this week?			
11				
12				
13				
14				
15				
16				
17				

Remember! Remember!

Before you start discussing an issue close to your heart, such as worthy causes or politics, research the facts as much as you can.

June

Date	What's on this week?			
18				
19				
20				
21				
22				
23				
24				

Remember! Remember!

Alchohol, smoking and drugs can all cause bad health and physical damage. Don't experiment with drugs or smoking, and always be responsible with alcohol.

June–July

Date	What's on this week?

25

26

27

28

29

30

1

Remember!
Remember!

Research careers and jobs that might interest you. Make the most of the exciting opportunities that are available and find a career path that interests you.

July

Date	What's on this week?	🍎	👟	🥛
2				
3				
4				
5				
6				
7				
8				

Remember! Remember!

Never let a part-time job interfere with your school work. A part-time job should be for extra money each week and not require too much of your time.

July

Date	What's on this week?			
9				
10				
11				
12				
13				
14				
15				

Remember! Remember!

After your exams you can continue your education or go straight into work. Both offer various opportunities. Do your research to decide what's best for you.

July

Date	What's on this week?			
16				
17				
18				
19				
20				
21				
22				

Remember! Remember!

The more calories you put in your body, the more energy you will need to burn off (through exercise) to prevent gaining too much extra weight.

July

Date	What's on this week?			
23				
24				
25				
26				
27				
28				
29				

**Remember!
Remember!**

You should aim to eat foods from each food group throughout the day. You should be sure to have fibre, proteins, dairy, sugar, fats, fruit and vegetables.

July–August

Date	What's on this week?			
30				
31				
1				
2				
3				
4				
5				

Remember! Remember!

A headache could be a sign of dehydration. Instead of taking a tablet to ease the pain, first drink a glass of water to see if the symptoms go away.

August

Date	What's on this week?			
6				
7				
8				
9				
10				
11				
12				

Remember! Remember!

If you suspect that a friend has trouble with their eating habits or is obsessed with their weight, try talking to them to see if it's likely to be a serious problem.

August

Date	What's on this week?			
13				
14				
15				
16				
17				
18				
19				

Remember! Remember!

Exercise is not only good for keeping your weight down, it also promotes good cardiovascular (heart) fitness and increases your overall health.

August

Date	What's on this week?	

20

21

22

23

24

25

26

Remember! Remember!

Grab some mates and get them to join you in your favourite sports activity. Head for the tennis court, local swimming pools, or the park with your rollerblades!

August–September

Date	What's on this week?			
27				
28				
29				
30				
31				
1				
2				

Remember! Remember!

When blowdrying your hair, be gentle with it. Don't scrub it dry with a towel, and dry it one section at a time using a cooler setting on your dryer.

September

Date	What's on this week?			
3				
4				
5				
6				
7				
8				
9				

Remember! Remember!

Treat your feet to some care and attention at least once a week. Rub hard patches with a pumice stone or body brush and massage lotion in to soothe the skin.

September

Date	What's on this week?				
10					
11					
12					
13					
14					
15					
16					

Remember! Remember!

Think positive! If you're feeling down about things, try to look on the bright side, or think of things that make you happy to lift your spirits.

September

Date	What's on this week?			
17				
18				
19				
20				
21				
22				
23				

Remember! Remember!

Hormones during puberty can create emotional turmoil! If you're getting overwhelmed by your emotions, speak to someone. A problem shared...

September

Date	What's on this week?				
24					
25					
26					
27					
28					
29					
30					

Remember! Remember!

Look after your teeth by brushing them at least twice a day and flossing regularly to prevent gum disease and the build-up of plaque.

October

Date	What's on this week?				
1					
2					
3					
4					
5					
6					
7					

Remember!
Remember!

As soon as you start to develop breasts, invest in a decent bra. It will be more comfortable and will support them, preventing the surrounding tissue from stretching.

October

Date	What's on this week?			
8				
9				
10				
11				
12				
13				
14				

Remember! Remember!

If you're passionate about a cause, try joining their organization. You can get involved in charity events or join youth groups to meet like-minded people.

October

Date	What's on this week?			
15				
16				
17				
18				
19				
20				
21				

Remember! Remember!

Be aware of your personal safety at all times. Never walk home alone at night or stay in situations that unnerve you, such as empty train carriages.

October

Date	What's on this week?			
22				
23				
24				
25				
26				
27				
28				

Remember! Remember!

Drinking and drugs not only harm your health, they can also lead to illegal and antisocial behaviour. The possession or taking of drugs can go on your permanent record.

October–November

Date	What's on this week?			
29				
30				
31				
1				
2				
3				
4				
5				

november

Date	What's on this week?			
6				
7				
8				
q				
10				
11				
12				

Remember! Remember!

To avoid the humiliation of being overheard, don't bitch and gossip about people! It won't do any good and being overheard could have unpleasant consequences.

november

Date	What's on this week?
13	
14	
15	
16	
17	
18	
19	

Remember! Remember!

Before you agree to a part-time job, ensure that you can get there and back safely. If you'll be travelling after dark, make sure a parent or guardian can pick you up.

november

Date	What's on this week?			
20				
21				
22				
23				
24				
25				
26				

Remember! Remember!

In this day and age, girls have the same opportunities as men, so take advantage of these modern attitudes to grab any career or education that suits you.

November–December

Date	What's on this week?			
27				
28				
29				
30				
1				
2				
3				

Remember! Remember!

If you find a career that you're interested in, ask around for more advice. Better still, if you know someone who already has that job, ask them for further information.

December

Date	What's on this week?			
4				
5				
6				
7				
8				
9				
10				

Remember! Remember!

Consider carefully before deciding on a career path. Take into account your likes, dislikes, strengths and weaknesses before choosing.

December

Date	What's on this week?	
11		
12		
13		
14		
15		
16		
17		

Remember! Remember!

Following a balanced, varied and nutritional diet should mean that you don't need to diet on low-fat or low-sugar foods.

December

Date	What's on this week?			
18				
19				
20				
21				
22				
23				
24				

Remember!
Remember!

Eat little and often during the day to maintain your blood sugar levels. Don't skip meals or eat irresponsibly. This could have the opposite effect to the one desired.

December

Date	What's on this week?			
25				
26				
27				
28				
29				
30				
31				

Remember! Remember!

Don't overstretch or push yourself when exercising. Pain isn't always good during exercise, it could be the sign of an injury rather than just tiredness.

Addresses

❀ Name:
✉ Address:
....
....
☎ Tel:
@ email:
🎁 Birthday:

❀ Name:
✉ Address:
....
....
☎ Tel:
@ email:
🎁 Birthday:

❀ Name:
✉ Address:
....
....
☎ Tel:
@ email:
🎁 Birthday:

❀ Name:
✉ Address:
....
....
☎ Tel:
@ email:
🎁 Birthday:

❀ Name:
✉ Address:
....
....
☎ Tel:
@ email:
🎁 Birthday:

❀ Name:
✉ Address:
....
....
☎ Tel:
@ email:
🎁 Birthday:

❀ Name:
✉ Address:
....
....
☎ Tel:
@ email:
🎁 Birthday:

❀ Name:
✉ Address:
....
....
☎ Tel:
@ email:
🎁 Birthday:

❀ Name:
✉ Address:
....
....
☎ Tel:
@ email:
🎁 Birthday:

❀ Name:
✉ Address:
....
....
☎ Tel:
@ email:
🎁 Birthday:

Name:

Address:

Tel:

@ email:

Birthday:

Name:

Address:

Tel:

@ email:

Birthday:

Name:

Address:

Tel:

@ email:

Birthday:

Name:

Address:

Tel:

@ email:

Birthday:

Name:

Address:

Tel:

@ email:

Birthday:

Name:

Address:

Tel:

@ email:

Birthday:

Name:

Address:

Tel:

@ email:

Birthday:

Name:

Address:

Tel:

@ email:

Birthday:

Addresses

❀ Name:
✉ Address:

☎ Tel:
@ email:
🎁 Birthday:

❀ Name:
✉ Address:

☎ Tel:
@ email:
🎁 Birthday:

❀ Name:
✉ Address:

☎ Tel:
@ email:
🎁 Birthday:

❀ Name:
✉ Address:

☎ Tel:
@ email:
🎁 Birthday:

❀ Name:
✉ Address:

☎ Tel:
@ email:
🎁 Birthday:

❀ Name:
✉ Address:

☎ Tel:
@ email:
🎁 Birthday:

❀ Name:
✉ Address:

☎ Tel:
@ email:
🎁 Birthday:

❀ Name:
✉ Address:

☎ Tel:
@ email:
🎁 Birthday:

❀ Name:
✉ Address:

☎ Tel:
@ email:
🎁 Birthday:

❀ Name:
✉ Address:

☎ Tel:
@ email:
🎁 Birthday:

Name:

Address:

Tel:

email:

Birthday:

Name:

Address:

Tel:

email:

Birthday:

Name:

Address:

Tel:

email:

Birthday:

Name:

Address:

Tel:

email:

Birthday:

Name:

Address:

Tel:

email:

Birthday:

Name:

Address:

Tel:

email:

Birthday:

Name:

Address:

Tel:

email:

Birthday:

Name:

Address:

Tel:

email:

Birthday:

Name:

Address:

Tel:

email:

Birthday:

Name:

Address:

Tel:

email:

Birthday:

Glossary

Acne
A skin complaint caused by hormonal changes, which produce more oil. This oil can block the pores and cause infection.

Apprenticeship
Learning a trade or profession by working with people who are qualified or skilled.

Bone density
How porous, or weak, your bones are. Calcium increases bone density.

Caffeine
A stimulant that occurs naturally in tea and coffee, and is added to drinks, such as cola.

Calcium
A metallic element that is an essential part of your bones and teeth.

Calorie
A measurement of heat, which shows how much energy foods produce when eaten.

Carbohydrate
An important source of energy found in foods, such as sugars and starches (for example, potatoes and pasta).

Cardiovascular
Cardiovascular exercise strengthens the heart and blood vessels.

Cholesterol
A fat-like substance found in your muscles and body tissue. Too much of it can be bad for your heart.

Cuticle
The small curve of skin that protects the bottom of your fingernails.

Dehydration
A dangerous lack of water in your body, leading to headaches and other symptoms.

Diabetes
A medical condition where a person has too much glucose, or sugar, in their blood. Symptoms include thirst, weight loss, excess urination and tiredness.

Diet
A way of eating. A 'healthy diet' takes in a balance of the food groups. Many diets are 'weight loss diets', usually recommended for people with serious obesity problems.

Eating disorder
Serious problems linked to eating habits, for example anorexia nervosa, bulimia nervosa and binge-eating disorder.

Fibre
Mostly indigestible material in food, which keeps your intestine operating properly.

Hormones
The body's chemical 'messengers', which pass on instructions to body tissues and organs. They usually set in motion bodily changes and can be linked to secondary functions, such as emotions and weight.

Insulin
A protein hormone, which helps to regulate the amount of glucose in the blood.

Junk food
Food with low nutritional value. It is often in the form of ready-meals or food from fast-food restaurants.

Low-impact
Exercise that avoids running, kicking and jumping, to minimize damage to joints.

Menstruation
Your monthly 'period' when your body releases blood that was used to line the womb in preparation for pregnancy.

Minerals
A vital element in your body, for example your bones, teeth, muscles and blood. You also need minerals in your diet to enable your body to use vitamins effectively.

Muscles
Tissue that makes your limbs and organs move, through expansion and contraction.

Nutrition
The intake of nutrients (nourishing substances) and how your body uses them.

Obesity
Being excessively overweight, to the point that your health is put in danger.

Oestrogen
A chiefly female hormone that stimulates changes in your body, for example to prepare your body for having babies.

Organic
Grown without the use of chemicals.

Organs
Your body's main functioning parts, such as the eyes, brain, heart, liver and so on.

Plaque
A thin coating of bacteria on your teeth that can cause tooth decay or gum disease.

Protein
Essential chemical compounds that help your body function. They can be found in meat, eggs, dairy products and beans.

Psychologist
A scientist who studies human behaviour, to understand a person's feelings or actions.

Puberty
The time when a child's body changes to allow reproduction (having babies).

Saturated fat
A fat from animals or dairy products, and selected vegetables (for example coconuts). It's often solid at room temperature and can raise your body's cholesterol levels.

Sprain
A joint injury caused by sudden twisting or wrenching of the ligaments.

Stamina
Energy, strength and resilience kept up over a period of time.

Sun Protection Factor (SPF)
The strength of your suntan lotion. For example, SPF15 enables you to stay in the sun 15 times longer than if you wore no sunscreen, before your skin starts to burn.

Testosterone
A hormone linked to masculine functions, such as muscle-building and making sperm.

Unsaturated fat
A fat that is usually liquid at room temperature, such as vegetable oil. Usually found in nuts, olives, avocado and fatty fish (for example, salmon).

UVA
Ultraviolet radiation. Dangerous to the skin, and causes long-term ageing effects, such as wrinkles.

UVB
Ultraviolet radiation. Dangerous to the skin in the short-term (sunburn) and long-term (skin cancer).

Vitamins
Groups of substances that are essential for your body to function properly. They occur naturally in certain foods and are taken into your body when you eat these foods.

Index

Index

The publishers wish to thank the following artists who have contributed to this book:
Louisa Leitao, Maltings

The publishers wish to thank the following photographer and models who contributed to this book:
Photographer: Trevor Clifford; Models: Amy Adams, Rose Arkell, Becky Evans, Miriam Evans
Alice Mcghee, Louisa Leitao, Laura Nundram, Ashleigh Smith, Laura Smith, Maria Tennant
Cover: Charlotte Marshall

The publishers wish to thank the following sources for the images used in this book:
11 (t/l) David Pollack/CORBIS; 22 (t/r) Franco Vogt/CORBIS; 23 (b/r) Mike McGill/CORBIS
24 (t/r) Neal Preston/CORBIS; 26 (c/l) Mark A. Johnson/CORBIS; 36 (t/r) Jonathan Cavendish/CORBIS
50 (b/l) Françoise Gervais/CORBIS; 61 (t/l) Larry Williams/CORBIS

All other photographs are from:
Hemera, Photodisc